Jeffrey,

I hope this will make you further open to the wonders of God's signs of love which surround you. One of the loveliest I know of is, happily, now a deacon. Many congratulations!

John Pinette

Signs
Words & Gestures

IN
every new situation
we must start all over again
like children,
cultivate a passionate interest
in things and events,
and begin by taking delight in externals,
until we have the good fortune
to grasp the substance.

JOHANN WOLFGANG VON GOETHE
1829
Wilhelm Meisters Wanderjahre I, 3

Signs
Words & Gestures

SHORT HOMILIES ON THE LITURGY

BALTHASAR FISCHER

*Translated
by
Matthew J. O'Connell
with
block prints by Helen Siegl*

PUEBLO PUBLISHING COMPANY
New York

Design: Br. Aelred Shanley

Originally published in German as *Von der Schale bis zum Kern* © 1979 Verlag Herder.

Scriptural pericopes quoted from the Revised Standard Version.

Excerpts from the English translation of The Roman Missal copyright © 1973, International Committee on English in the Liturgy, Inc. All rights reserved.

English translation © 1981 Pueblo Publishing Co., Inc. 1860 Broadway, New York, N.Y. 10023. All rights reserved.

Printed in the United States of America.

ISBN: 0-916134-48-2

CONTENTS

FOREWORD

BALTHASAR FISCHER is perhaps best known to the wider public in this country for a small booklet on liturgical renewal published in 1958, *Questions the Catechism Didn't Answer.* He has also lectured at Notre Dame and at St. John's University in New York City. In the international academic world he is widely regarded as the foremost liturgical scholar alive today. Acclaimed as the outstanding pupil of the famous Josef A. Jungmann, Dr. Fischer has been a professor at the Theological Faculty of Trier since 1947. His early pioneering efforts at liturgical renewal were rewarded in 1961 when he was named a consultor to the Congregation for Sacraments and Worship. In addition to helping frame the Constitution on the Sacred Liturgy of Vatican II, he served as chairperson of the committee entrusted with the reform of the rite of baptism for children and the restored rite of Christian initiation of adults. Appropriately, on the occasion of his sixtieth birthday he was honored by a *Festschrift* of papers from his peers devoted to the study of baptism.

He is the author of almost 200 articles, many of which treat of the relationship between liturgy and popular piety. After all, he began his ministry as a parish priest and his first professorial duties were those of a homiletics professor. This pastoral sensitivity is evidenced in these short homilies which bring home to the members of the worshiping assembly the inner meaning of the ritual actions and words they celebrate. Indeed, this profound respect for religious affectivity could well be the missing piece in the liturgical renewal today.

Fr. Fischer lives what he preaches. He conducts a weekly Mass for children; an expertise which found expression in the *Directory for Masses with Children* and is further reflected in this volume. He is also a faithful visitor to the sick in the hospitals of Trier. Moreover, his generosity and vision have been experienced by over thirty doctoral candidates whose dissertations he directed, including Aidan Kavanagh, John Gallen, Mark Searle, and John McKenna in this country. As one of those fortunate people who can claim him as a *Doktorvater* it is a distinct privilege to introduce *Signs, Words, and Gestures* to the English-speaking world.

CHARLES W. GUSMER
Darlington Seminary

THE ROMAN LITURGY is very ancient, and yet we find ourselves in a new situation now that we are celebrating it in a revised and vernacular form as a result of the Second Vatican Council. This new situation proves again the wisdom of the eighty-year old Johann Wolfgang von Goethe, from whom the quotation on the title page of this book is taken.

The first reaction to the Council was an almost childlike enjoyment of the new externals. Not for a long time had the outward form of the liturgy been so much the focus of interest as it was in the fifteen years after the *Constitution on the Liturgy* was promulgated on December 4, 1963, as the first fruits of the Council. Since the beginning of the seventies, however, this first "childhood phase" seems to have been left behind. Many, especially among the young, feel a growing desire to pass from externals to substance. There is a feeling abroad that we have spent enough time playing with novelties and must begin to draw spiritual life from what has been attained.

As a result, terms like liturgical piety and liturgical spirituality have suddenly acquired a new prestige all over the world.

It is my hope that on this journey from externals to substance this little book may provide a modest service. It is meant as an unpretentious aid, readable by the ordinary Christian, in the effort to pass from the externals of liturgical words and signs and gestures (be they of ancient origin or the result of the reform) to the substance which is a sound liturgical spirituality.

A glance at the table of contents will be enough to show that I have not approached the subject systematically. I have simply taken, almost at random, twenty of the countless signs, gestures, and words on which something might be said.

I do not want the children to be forgotten, since the journey from externals to substance cannot be begun too early. Therefore, as the last part of the book I have added ten talks to elementary school children; these too deal in their own way with liturgical signs, gestures, and words. They are intended not least as a stimulus to those who would like to discuss with their children, at home, the liturgy with which these children will become familiar.

Two-thirds of the thirty subjects have to do with the Mass. Perhaps they will encourage those homilists who are recognizing with increasing clarity the soundness of the advice given by the authors of the *General Instruction of the Roman Missal* when, in Article 41, they suggest that not only the readings of the Mass but the Ordinary and Proper as well can be the subject of the Sunday homily. Anyone who has preached on such topics knows the typical reaction of even the best of the faithful: "Why did no one ever tell us that?"

The eighty-year old Goethe speaks of the good fortune of grasping the substance; this is a worldly idiom for what we call grace. Neither one—good fortune or grace—can be attained by our own powers; both are gifts from the heavenly Father, as John 6.44 implies.

The more that the members of the Church, be they children or adults, are led by the Spirit of God to grasp the substance of the liturgy, or at least are on their way to this goal, the more vital and joyous will the liturgy be in the final years of this millennium, even if the world in which we celebrate becomes an ever colder place.

BALTHASAR FISCHER
Trier, September 2, 1979

I am baptized.
Christ is my Lord.
I belong to him.

1

SEALED WITH THE SEAL OF THE CROSS

AMONG THE MOST striking innovations in the celebration of infant baptism is the practice of having the parents (and, if it seems appropriate, the godparents as well) make the sign of the cross on the foreheads of the little candidates, after the celebrant has done so. What is the meaning of this sign of the cross that is made at the beginning of the baptismal rite? Why do the parents join in making it?

According to a custom that is as old as the human race, a sign carried on the forehead is a sign of belonging. Slaves, especially, often had such a sign branded on their foreheads (or arms); it told others who their owner was. In the sacrament of baptism Jesus who suffered and died and conquered on the cross takes possession of the children whom their parents have brought to him. The children will belong to him not as slaves used to belong to their masters, but they will belong to Christ the way lovers belong to each other.

It is, then, a deeply meaningful innovation that at this point in the baptismal liturgy the child's parents, in particular, should join the Church in making this sign of possession. They will be doing it repeatedly later on when, following a fine old custom, they bless their child—especially the mother when she makes a small cross on the child's forehead before sleep. If we bear in mind the link with baptism, this silent maternal gesture suddenly becomes eloquent. In fact, it really deserves the name the early Christians gave it, for the mother "puts a seal" on her child; she renews the "sealing" that took place in baptism. She is saying: "You were baptized, my child. May he to whom you have belonged since then continue to protect you."

It is worth noting that through the centuries down to our own day mothers have made this sign of the cross in its original form, as attested as far back as the third century and as now restored in the baptismal liturgy: that is, with a single cross on the forehead. Later on, these children may sign themselves with a triple cross on forehead, mouth and breast, or may embrace forehead, shoulders and heart in a single large sign of the cross. In either case, the meaning is the same as when their mother signed them each night. But now these children will be saying to themselves as it were: "I am baptized. Christ is my Lord. I belong to him."

Isn't it marvelous that we can say of a baptized child: This child will live and die as one sealed with the sign of the cross; at the end this child will take refuge in him who is stronger than death and all the powers of darkness! Parents cannot remain permanently with their children, but the Lord will be with them all days. And some day he will lead his "sealed" followers through death to the indestructible life of those who are in the Father's house with Christ for all eternity.

Source of life,
which gushed from
the wound of Christ

2

THE SIGN OF WATER

WHY DID THE Lord use the sign of water in instituting the basic sacrament by which he wills to take possession of us? In order to answer this question, we must first know something about the original form of water baptism since our present practice of pouring water on the child's head, though adequate for a valid baptism, is no longer the full sign of baptism.

It was thought for a long time that the full sign consisted of a triple complete immersion of an adult candidate who had removed his or her clothing and descended into the piscina or pool of water; in Europe during the Middle Ages, for example (and even today in Russia), they had the candidates undress and then immersed them completely in the baptismal font. (Our word "baptism" is derived from the Greek verb *baptizein*, "to dip, plunge, immerse.") This method of

3

baptizing was intended to imitate a death by drowning and a rescue from this death, thus expressing in a symbolic way the fact that to be baptized is to be buried with Christ so that we may then be raised up with him to new life (Romans 6.4).

Admittedly, this is indeed the idea behind the baptism of children by immersion. But it is no longer possible today to maintain that this was the sole form of baptism in the early Church. Too many early Christian fonts have been discovered which are so shallow that an adult standing upright in them was by no means immersed.

We must therefore, in all probability, think of baptism as having taken a different form in the early Church.

After each of the three affirmations of faith, the one baptizing poured water over the candidates as they stood in water to their waists. But the water was poured in such volume that the candidates were robed, so to speak, in a cloak of water. Consequently, the rite could be called a baptismal bath as compared with our present method.

It is against this background that we must answer the question with which we began. The concern in this kind of bath is not primarily to wash away dirt but to refresh and revitalize. The Germans have an expression that is worth recalling at this point. After bathing in a river on a hot summer afternoon (in prepollution days) the common saying, when coming out of the water was: I feel "reborn." That is precisely the effect of the baptismal bath, but in a much deeper sense: we are reborn of water and the Holy Spirit.

The ancients had a marvelous image to express the special efficacy of the baptismal bath, an image based on the biblical account of the water that flowed from the side of the crucified Christ (John 19.34). To be baptized is, they said, to be immersed in the life-giving and redemptive stream of water from the pierced side of the Savior; it is to be caught up in the redemption that flows from the cross of Christ.

4   In the most venerable baptismal church of the West—the

baptistery of the Lateran Basilica in Rome—high above the font through which adult candidates for baptism once passed, there is a fifth-century inscription that runs around the wall. It speaks of the baptismal water that waits below for the candidates. The inscription reads: "Here is the source of life, which gushed from the wound of Christ and washes the whole universe."

We are
the aroma of Christ

3

ANOINTED ON THE FOREHEAD
WITH CHRISM

I F WE ARE to understand the anointing on the forehead that is part of confirmation, we must relate it to the other sacramental anointings. In the anointing with the oil of catechumens before baptism it is the breast that is anointed. This is all that remains of an ancient anointing of the entire body which the candidate for baptism in the early Church understood to be an anointing for combat. The candidate needed no lengthy explanation of this point since athletes coated themselves with oil before contests in the arena. Those who were to be baptized would not be leaving the struggle with Satan behind them but on the contrary had to expect its continuation.

The anointing that follows upon the baptismal act is an anointing with chrism on the crown of the head. This recalls not the arena but the anointing of kings in the Old

Testament. The person who is baptized now shares in the royal priesthood of Christ; this anointing on the crown of the head is a sign of what we now call the "common priesthood of the baptized."

The two anointings in baptism are followed by a third in confirmation. This too is done with chrism, but another part of the body—the forehead—has been chosen for the new anointing. The choice is explained by the element of public manifestion that attaches to confirmation. Baptism is to confirmation as Easter is to Pentecost. On Pentecost the event that had taken place on Easter was made public and reached out to influence the world. So too, as a result of confirmation and its new gift of the Spirit the event which takes place in baptism begins to affect the Church in a public way "in the form of an open confession of Christ and of service to our fellow human beings," as one synod of bishops puts it. This is the reason why among us Western Christians the bishop is usually the one who administers confirmation, for he represents the general public of the local Church in which the baptized are henceforth to bear witness to what they are.

In confirmation, then, the sign of Christ is traced on the part of the body that is most immediately visible to anyone who meets us. Nothing is more difficult for us to hide than that which is in any way written on our forehead. Anyone who has ever had to wear even a small bandaid on the forehead after a mishap can attest to the truth of what I am saying!

It is no accident that the one confirming uses oil in tracing the sign of the cross on the forehead. Confirmation is a new sealing with the Holy Spirit so that the recipient may bear witness before the world. Now the ancients saw oil as a special symbol of the Spirit. Our forefathers took a more contemplative approach to these matters and found greater pleasure in images than we do. In their eyes, the olive tree was an image of the Father, its fruit was an image of the Son, and, therefore, the oil—that which flows out in all directions as the ultimate and purest extract of tree and fruit—became for them a symbol of the Spirit.

7

It is also no accident that chrism, the noblest of the three oils, should be used for the sign of the cross in confirmation. Chrism is produced by adding aromatic essences (especially balsam) to olive oil. Here again the element of public manifestation that is proper to confirmation exercises its influence. Paul says of Christians that they should be "the aroma of Christ" (2 Corinthians 2.14). Wherever Christians live their baptism and confirmation in an authentic way, they emit as it were a "strong and wholesome fragrance."

How can anyone observe Mother Teresa at work serving the starving children of Calcutta and not smell something of this strong and wholesome fragrance, this "aroma of Christ"? This woman has translated into action what the bishop meant when on the day of her confirmation he laid his hand on her head and anointed her forehead so that she might confess her faith and bear witness to it.

*God,
the Father of mercies . . .
give you
pardon
and peace*

4

ABSOLUTION WITH HANDS EXTENDED

THE REFORM OF the sacramental rite of penance has restored a gesture that is very old and very eloquent. When a confession is heard in a reconciliation room, as is possible nowadays, the priest extends both hands, or at least the right hand over the penitent's head at the absolution. The practice, approved by the new ritual, is a version of the ancient Christian custom of laying both hands on the penitent's head. Even when the confessional box had been introduced and the gesture of which I am speaking had been rendered impossible, it was not wholly forgotten. In the old ritual for sacramental penance the confessor behind the grill was told to extend his right hand toward the penitent. This was actually a vestige of the ancient laying on of hands, but it had become hardly recognizable and gave the impression that the priest was simply raising his hand for the sign of the cross that also accompanied the absolution.

It is remarkable how the great gesture of the imposition or laying on of hands changes its meaning according to the context in which it is used, without there being any need of expressly calling attention to the change. If we enter a cathedral and see the bishop laying hands on the head of one young man after another, we do not get the idea that his intention is to console them or forgive their sins; rather we immediately sense that the gesture symbolizes the communication of spiritual authority. And if we attend the celebration of an anointing of the sick in the new rite during the eucharist and see how before the anointing the priest passes from one sick person to another and silently lays his hands on the head of each, we understand that the gesture here symbolizes the reassuring and consoling power that goes forth from the sacrament of anointing of the sick.

The imposition of hands on the sick is akin to the imposition of hands in the sacrament of penance at the absolution. There is no greater consolation under heaven than the unparalleled gift here given in the name of Christ: the forgiveness of sins. The new formula of absolution, which the priest pronounces with hands extended, begins with these words: "God, the Father of mercies, through the death and resurrection of his Son has reconciled the world to himself."

The next words express most clearly perhaps the meaning of the laying on of hands here: "through the ministry of the Church may God give you pardon and peace."

A basic pattern has finally come to light here once again, and its message hits home to anyone who has retained a feeling for the language of gestures. But does this mean that we should simply get rid of the confessional ("the box") which many find such an uncongenial piece of furniture? Luckily, such a hasty and unpastoral conclusion has not been drawn. For, while there are indeed individuals (a growing number of them, it seems) who find the confessional a hindrance to their confession, there are also, and always will be, others who seek and need the anonymity of the confessional if they are to confess their sins. Complete freedom of choice must be preserved in this area.

The person who chooses the reconciliation room experiences, like all those who receive the sacrament of penance in the individual form, the fact that forgiveness is pronounced "upon his or her head"; this is the unique advantage which individual sacramental absolution has over all other forms of the forgiveness of sins.

Lord,
ease their sufferings

5

SOOTHING OIL AS SIGN IN THE
ANOINTING OF THE SICK

THANKS BE to God that since the postconciliar reform of the sacrament of the sick there are evidently fewer and fewer Catholics who shrink in fear from this sacrament, as they so often did in the past. The old, fear-inspiring notion of a "last" anointing which one received when all hope was gone, was false. The anointing of the sick is the consoling sacrament which the Lord has instituted for the seriously ill and in which he draws close to them during the critical period which any serious illness represents for even the most devout person. The most important words we hear in the administration of this sacrament are present in the Bible itself, in the Letter of James which speaks of our sacrament for the first time. The words are: "May the Lord . . . raise you up" (cf. James 5.15). It is for the Lord to decide whether indeed to raise up the sick so that they may return to their everyday lives, but in every case the Lord will raise them up interiorly and strengthen and console them.

Why has oil been used as the sign in this sacrament ever since biblical times? In the ancient world and in ours as well, to apply oil to the body of one who is ill is to ease its suffering. After all, what do we do when we have been burned? We apply a salve to the painful spot. This salve may be any one of the many available in a modern pharmacy, but its basic component is still oil. Then suddenly the skin ceases to burn so much. The salve has eased the pain, and we breathe a sigh of relief.

This experience shows us the meaning of the anointing of the sick. This sacrament is intended not as a preparation for death (oil would be a poor sign for such a purpose) but as an alleviation of suffering. In the prayer of thanksgiving over the oil of the sick (a prayer which, in the new ritual, is a part of every administration of the sacrament), the priest says: "Lord God, with faith in you our brother (sister) will be anointed with this holy oil. Ease his (her) sufferings and strength his (her) weakness."

In addition, when consecrating this oil on Holy Thursday (or a few days before) in the mother church of the diocese, the bishop has already asked that this oil might have power to do away with suffering. It is not the oil itself, of course, but Christ who, through the sign of oil, grants alleviation by the power of his Spirit, so that the sick person may breathe easily again.

There is another important point: the marking of the forehead and hands with the holy oil may be done in the form of a cross even if the rubrics of the new rite don't provide that expressly anymore. The use of this sign has become so familiar in this context that we no longer reflect much on it. And yet something basic is being expressed here. All the sacraments, this one included, come from the cross of Christ. The power of the Spirit streamed forth as it were, and continues to stream forth, from the wound in the

Redeemer's heart that was laid open for us. This power takes hold of us in the sacraments. In the sacrament of which we are now speaking it is the power Christians need when their way leads through the darkness of suffering. There is a prayer we like to use after receiving holy communion, but it is one that a sick person may with special appropriateness address to Christ after receiving the anointing of the sick: "Even though I walk through the valley of the shadow of death, I fear no evil; for thou art with me" (Psalm 23.4).

Representatives of the hands of Christ

6

TWO HANDS ANOINTED WITH CHRISM

AT AN ORDINATION to the priesthood, after the sacramental rite proper, which by the Master's will consists of an imposition of hands and a prayer, the newly ordained are robed in the vestments for Mass. Then the bishop has them come before him once again. They extend both hands to him, palms up, and he anoints them in the form of a large cross which runs from the thumb of the left hand to the index finger of the right, and from the thumb of the right hand to the index finger of the left. As the bishop traces this sign he says: "The Father anointed our Lord Jesus Christ through the power of the Holy Spirit. May Jesus preserve you to sanctify the Christian people and to offer sacrifice to God."

The bishop is here engaging in a kind of short catechetical play. His purpose is to make clear to the newly ordained and   15 to the entire congregation the area in which the role of these newly ordained men as other Christs in the midst of God's people will be most perceptible. That area is the priest's hands. These are to represent the "holy and venerable hands" of the Master that were extended over the table in the supper room and on the wood of the cross in the gesture of sacrifice and blessing. Therefore by means of the Greek letter *chi* (which is shaped like our X) and of the chrism the hands of these men are branded as it were with the name that begins with the letter *chi* and means "Anointed One" in an unqualified sense: that is, the name of Christ.

The new formula that now accompanies the act of anointing makes it seem that blessing ("sanctify the Christian people") is the primary task of these hands. But the rite that immediately follows upon the anointing of the hands corrects this impression. For in the anointed hands of each newly ordained priest the bishop places a paten with hosts on it and a chalice, and says: "Accept from the holy people of God the gifts to be offered to him. Know what you are doing, and imitate the mystery you celebrate: model your life on the mystery of the Lord's cross."

These hands exist, then, in order to raise up in a visible manner the transformed gifts of the people. They are hands that bless only in the sense that they are to distribute the fruits of this redemptive sacrifice. There is no priestly blessing that is not given by the sign of the cross.

In the last analysis the New Testament knows only a single priest. Any human priest is, in the words of John Chrysostom, nothing but the outstretched arm of Christ that seeks to reach all times and all regions of the world. The sacrificing, blessing hands of Christ are represented among men and women by the hands of their fellow men and fellow sinners. It is these hands that are to make the Redeemer's legacy constantly available to the faithful and to distribute its riches.

It is no accident that the newly ordained priest is told in this context that he must model his life on the mystery of the cross. It is impossible to talk of the hands of Christ without thinking of the fact that they were pierced with agony on the cross. The Rhenish liturgical scholar Rupert of Deutz († 1129/30), in whose time the priest's hands were anointed with two small crosses on the palms, tells us that this spot was chosen as a reminder to the young priest of the nails which left a mark for all eternity on the Master's hands. The priest can render his service only if he places his life under the sign of the cross.

Take this ring
as a sign of
my love and fidelity

7

TWO HANDS JOINED

THE PRIEST'S chrism-anointed hands, which are permitted to work among human beings as representatives of the pierced hands of the Master, would not exist if there had not first been two hands, designated in the same way with a sign of blessing. These are the hands of the newly ordained priest's parents. Since the hour of their marriage they wear the blessed wedding ring which they gave each other when they mutually committed themselves to each other in the name of God and in the power of the sacrament. Christian priesthood has its roots in Christian marriage and family.

I know a valley in the Austrian Tyrol; it retains an old practice which wonderfully brings to mind the deep connection between the sacraments of ordination and matrimony. Before the newly ordained priest offers his first holy Mass in the presence of the assembled village community his father and mother come to the altar. The son turns to these two members of the parish and in the breathless silence of the gathering two hands are raised, one after the other; they are hands with wedding rings. First the father's, then the mother's, hand is raised. They both trace the sign of the cross on the forehead of their priest son. The parents wish to say, "Now we give you, whom the Lord has given us as the fruit of our love, back to God entirely as his servant."

The custom of expressing the connection between engagement and marriage and the wearing of rings is older than Christianity. Indeed, for a long time it retained silent unchristian overtones in the Christian liturgy. For a long time the situation was such that only *one* ring was blessed at a marriage ceremony. It was the bride's ring which the groom put on her finger. It appeared as if the bride, as the weaker partner, needed the commitment more. During medieval times objections were raised to this custom. If the ring is a sign of a life-long commitment in love and fidelity, which receives the power of the sacrament in the marriage rite, then, indeed, a Christian marriage must express the mutuality of the commitment.

Thus it came about that, according to the newest liturgical reform, both partners exchange rings during this part of the marriage liturgy all over the world. The newly married groom gives a ring to the newly married bride and she gives a ring to the groom saying: "Take this ring as a sign of my love and fidelity. In the name of the Father, and the Son and of the Holy Spirit."

Newly married partners put the ring on each other's left hand. Only the Bishop wears his ring on the right hand. Here we notice an old popular belief which came from a medical fallacy but which expressed a deep truth about the wedding ring. People believed a blood vessel ran from the left hand's ring finger to the heart. Of course, the ring is associated with the heart. Whoever wears it wishes to say, "My heart belongs in inviolable fidelity to him who gave me this blessed ring as a sign of love and fidelity, just as his belongs to me."

"The priest wants to praise the altar"

8

KISSING THE ALTAR

THERE WERE surely people who thought that the reform of the Mass would do away with such "outmoded" gestures as kissing the altar. But, as everyone knows, this did not happen. The reform consisted rather in restoring the original practice of having the priest kiss the altar, not many times as had been customary, but only when greeting it and when leaving it at the end of the service.

We are always hearing that "modern men and women" cannot make head or tail of such a gesture. I decided, therefore, a number of years ago, to find out just how elementary school children, who had been told nothing about the meaning of the kiss given to the altar, were reacting to this sign. Well, the initial response to my question was a long, embarassed silence. Was the question perhaps too difficult for children of this age?

Then an eight-year-old boy raised his hand and gave an answer so simple and correct that even years later I find myself astonished at the unspoiled clarity of vision expressed in his response. The boy said: "The priest wants to praise the altar." The single word "praise" says precisely what the gesture meant to the age that introduced it. The priest is saying: There are many tables in the world around which families gather for meals, and they are all good, but there is one of them that must be praised above all other tables on our earth; the Lord's table, the table at which the Lord ever anew prepares his mysterious sacrificial meal and offers it to us.

There are, of course, cultures that are offended by the idea of kissing an object. Immediately after the Council priests in these circumstances received permission to touch the altar with their forehead instead of their lips, since this is a gesture of reverence with which these cultures are familiar. There was no need, however, to eliminate the kissing of the altar in a culture such as ours, in which, as we may see on television, the winner of a cup will kiss his trophy on receiving it. This gesture is one of those liturgical actions which many people are appreciating once again and of which they are thinking: "It's a good thing that in our excessively rationalistic world there should be this kind of wordless sign." It is one of the great discoveries of recent times—a discovery that, not by chance, has taken place especially in America—that human beings also communicate without words and by means of signs which do not require lengthy accompanying explanations.

The Catholic Chuch has always renowned for understanding the language of gestures. We should be glad that after a rigorous testing of her ancient liturgical gestures she has allowed the kissing of the altar to retain the place in the Mass that it has held for more than a thousand years.

We all feel, deep down, that what that young boy was trying to express is indeed true. The priest intends to "praise" the altar. By doing so, he makes us aware that the altar is more than a piece of liturgical furniture needed for Mass and that it is rather a place which every Christian must regard as holy and deserving of praise and love. It is not just any table, but the table of the Lord from which our real life is constantly fed.

*Let my prayer
be counted
like incense
before thee*

9

INCENSE

I N RECENT years we may have often heard our
Protestant friends saying in tones of regret: One of the
things I've always liked about your Catholic Church is
the way it speaks to the whole person and all the senses,
even the sense of smell. It's too bad that you've discon-
tinued the use of incense."

God be thanked that we can set the speaker straight on this
point. Talk of eliminating incense—like the more serious
talk of eliminating the saints—is a false alarm. The revised
liturgical books provide for incense in every case in which it
had been used in the past. This much is true, however: the
use of incense is no longer obligatory, but the reason for
making it optional is that it is no longer restricted to certain
solemn Masses but is permissible, in principle, in every
Mass. Unfortunately, some individuals have not gotten the

message and act as though incense has indeed been eliminated when in fact it is being promoted, but on a wider scale and therefore as option rather than obligation. We may well feel more strongly today than we did ten years ago, that the appeal to the whole person which has been characteristic of Catholic liturgy needs to be encouraged more than ever and that the implicit warning of well-intentioned Protestant friends should not be dismissed lightly.

There is a further reason for retaining incense. Anyone who has ever taken part in an Eastern rite liturgy knows how much more extensive a role the constantly swinging censer plays in it. Shall we deliberately abandon a tradition that still unites East and West (and that awakens nostalgia rather than repulsion in many Protestant Christians of our day)?

Such considerations, however, would not be enough to warrant the retention of incense if the custom served purely and simply to make the liturgy more festive and did not convey a special message of its own. But it does in fact have a specific meaning. Whenever a real "cloud of incense" rises from the censer (rarely enough, alas!), those present instinctively grasp the signification. The psalmist expressed it back in the Old Testament: "Let my prayer be counted like incense before thee" (Psalm 141.2). For example, the cloud of incense that envelops the altar and gifts at Mass and, in subsequent incensations, the priest and faithful as well, is a symbol of that atmosphere of prayer to which reference is made in the ancient summons spoken by the celebrant at the threshold of the inner sanctuary of the eucharist: *Sursum corda!* Lift up your hearts! Nothing is more important for the success of our liturgy than that we disentangle ourselves from the thicket of thoughts and cares which hold us prisoner, and make ourselves free for God. Symbolic human language in this area is based on the image of above and below, and no sign can give such simple and effective expression as incense does to the upward movement of adoration.

Incense at a grave, if circumstances allow its use there, has a somewhat different meaning. The meaning can be best understood from the old prayer (a victim of the reform) the celebrant spoke as he incensed the coffin after it had been placed in the ground: "May God—Father, Son, and Holy Spirit—delight your soul with heavenly fragrance." In this symbolic language heaven was seen as a great house of God that is filled with the fragrance of incense (and of what can the words "house of God" be more fittingly used than of heaven?); the wishes and prayers of relatives and friends at the grave were that the dead person might dwell forever in this house of God where all is adoration.

If it be true that incense is a sign of adoration, then it must continue to be used in an age of increasing awareness that adoration is the breath of life.

"We are beggars— that's the fact"

10

WITH EXTENDED HANDS

ISN'T IT really surprising that during his "presidential prayers" (the opening prayer or prayer of the day, the prayer over the gifts, and the concluding prayer) and especially during the eucharistic prayer, the priest at the altar should adopt a posture diametrically opposed to the one we learned on our mother's lap? We brought our hands together for prayer and clasped them or pressed them against one another. At the altar, however, the priest separates them and holds them up to God like two empty cups: he extends his hands.

These two gestures of prayer were introduced into a liturgy of the Mass at different periods; both are meaningful and legitimate. To join the hands is to signify that the usual daily activity of these hands ceases for a moment and the hands come into their own, and will be, as it were, taking a

26

holiday. Something like a holiday, after all, begins every time we start to pray.

But why does the priest do the opposite when he acts as president of the worshiping community and, in the name of all of us, pronounces the most important prayers of the Mass? Why does he extend his hands instead of bringing them together? This gesture is, in fact, older and more venerable that that of the joined hands; the latter came into use in the Mass as a gesture of prayer only in the Middle Ages, north of the Alps. But as early as the catacombs we find the Church or the soul represented as praying the way the priest and the faithful prayed at that time: with extended hands.

When hundreds of thousands of Eastern Christians went over to Islam, they took this gesture of prayer with them, and anyone who visits a mosque will see devout Muslims praying even today with extended hands, the way a Catholic priest does at Mass.

On one occasion I gained new insight into this ancient gesture, when I read somewhere that the Assyrians had a word for prayer which meant "to open the fist." The fist, and especially a fist raised threateningly, is the sign of a highhanded, even violent peron. People grasp things in closed hands when they are unwilling to let go of them; they use clenched fists to assault and hurt and, even worse, to beat others down so that they cannot get up.

Those who pray, however, are saying before God that they are renouncing all highhandedness, all pride in their own sufficiency, all violence. They open their fists. They hold up their empty hands to God: "I have nothing that I have not received from you, nothing that you have not placed in my empty hands. Therefore I do not keep a frantic hold on anything you have given me; therefore, too, I desire not to strike and hurt but only to give and to spread happiness and joy. For I myself am dependent on him who fills my empty hands with his gifts."

This old gesture of prayer, which the reform—thank God! 27

—has retained, is thus a whole sermon in itself. It is a sermon we must all take to heart, even if we ourselves no longer pray this way in public. For, at bottom, all of us extend empty hands to God when we pray.

The thought I am trying to convey here is summed up in the final words that Martin Luther is reported as having spoken when he was dying: "We are beggars—that's the fact."

*I saw water
flowing from
the right side
of the temple*

11

VIDI AQUAM

IN RECENT years many who attend Sunday Mass will
have been surprised to see the Mass once again
beginning with an action the reform was supposed to
have eliminated. I am referring to the "Sunday commemoration of baptism," which used to be known as the *Asperges*,
from the first Latin word of the song that used to accompany
it in the course of the Church year. But I want to speak here
of the special form which the Sunday commemoration of
baptism takes during the Easter season, when the accompanying Latin song begins with the words that provide the
title for this talk: *Vidi aquam*.

As the priest walks down the center aisle and sprinkles the
congregation with holy water, the congregation sings the
accompanying song for Easter season, and there is no

objection to their using the old Latin text. Much as we rejoice to use the vernacular in the liturgy and will allow no malcontent to take it from us, it is good nonetheless that the old supranational liturgical language should come into its own on such occasions, in the form of short texts to be sung by the faithful.

But the heart should know that the mouth is singing, and the faithful must be given a translation along with the Latin text. As soon as the *Vidi aquam* song is translated, the meaning of the entire ceremony will appear clearly. It will also be easier to understand why such a precious rite—in spite of being optional—should be retained. The Easter song for the Sunday commemoration of baptism is taken from the prophet Ezekiel's vision of the temple and reads as follows: "I saw water flowing from the right side of the temple, alleluia. It brought God's life and his salvation, and the people sang in joyful praise: alleluia, alleluia" (cf. Ezekiel 47.1-2, 9).

The Fathers of the Church interpreted these words of the prophet as referring to the stream of water that flowed from the side of Jesus on Golgotha as we saw when speaking about the sign of water. Jesus himself had compared his body to the temple, had he not? But this water that had its source in the redemptive suffering of the redeemer was in turn seen by the early Church as an image of the water of baptism. In the water of baptism the prophet's vision is fulfilled: "It brought God's life and his salvation."

The sprinkling with holy water on the "weekly Easter" is intended to be what its name implies: a weekly commemoration of baptism, a grateful remembrance of the fact that this redemptive water has reached us without our cooperation or merit.

Not without reason has this commemoration of baptism been placed at the beginning of the Sunday eucharist. For this eucharist is the thanksgiving feast of the baptized, of those who have been saved; an unbaptized person, however devout, can never be admitted under any circumstances to this mysterious table.

One of our students of theology who returned home from World War II in 1945 told me that on one occasion, when he was a soldier in the far north of Finland, he wanted to attend the Sunday eucharist of an Orthodox community: not as a communicant (this was still unthinkable at that time), but as a respectful onlooker. The priest wanted to prevent the uniformed young man (with whom verbal communication was not possible) from entering the church, until the latter took courage, dipped his hand in the holy water font, and covered all his face with holy water. The priest immediately realized that the German soldier was a baptized Christian and let him enter.

We may do more than enter. The table awaits us at which our baptismal life is fed over and over again. We have every reason to cry out in gratitude: alleluia, alleluia!

"This prayer
can express everything"

12

KYRIE, ELEISON

OW MANY hundreds of times have we not all prayed at the beginning of Mass: "Lord, have mercy! Christ, have mercy!" and yet, to be honest, how little, on the whole, we have reflected on what we were saying!

Such short prayers have a unique power, but they are also open to a special danger: they can readily come to the lips without passing through the heart. And yet this very ancient cry for mercy in our liturgy is a kind of primordial prayer that we must stop and reflect on a little.

To reflect on this prayer is, above all, to consider what it means to call upon Christ as LORD. The Greek form, which we used to recite, is: *Kyrie, eleison, Kyrios* being the word chosen by the Greek translators of the Old Testament as the equivalent of Yahweh, the Hebrew name for God. When addressed to Christ, the word amounts to a grateful, laudatory confession of the divinity of him who by dying conquered death; it was a confession that could cost people their lives during the early persecutions.

We find, then, that even so very brief a prayer as this follows the general rule that praise and thanksgiving come first and the petition flows from these. Because you are our Lord, who has passed victoriously through death to life, therefore we pray you: Have mercy on us and on the whole world. The petition means more than "Help us!" It means: "Take all of us with you on your journey through death to life."

If we interpret the *Kyrie, eleison* in this way, we can understand how one of the great spiritual men of the East, Nicholas Cabasilas, could say, back in the fourteenth century: "This prayer can express everything at once." Cabasilas meant that it is really enough simply to commend ourselves, our dear ones, and the whole world to the redeeming mercy of him who died and rose for us.

For this reason, every time we stand at the threshold of holy Mass, in which this mercy is celebrated and comes to us in "bodily" form, we cry out: *Kyrie, eleison.* It is not an accident that the same cry is repeated at the breaking of the bread just before communion: "Lamb of God, you take away the sins of the world; have mercy on us."

In the East there are believers who do more than say this prayer. They take it with them from the liturgical celebration and make it a constant prayer of the heart. I shall never forget the monk Habakkuk of Mount Athos, and the love that radiated from within him. You could see the old man's lips moving as he spoke the Jesus Prayer: "Jesus, Son of David, have mercy on me." I am convinced that as he prayed, he was not thinking only of himself, and that his intention was to commend all of us and the entire world to the loving mercy of the Redeemer.

Even if Christians of the West do not repeat this prayer unceasingly, it may well spring to our lips in everyday life: Lord, have mercy on him! Lord, have mercy on her! Lord, have mercy on them! For you died and rose from the dead for the sake of all human beings.

33

*Lovers praise
each other*

13

WE WORSHIP YOU,
WE GIVE YOU THANKS,
WE PRAISE YOU FOR YOUR GLORY

THE GLORIA of the Mass is one of the pearls in the treasure of liturgical prayers. Whole generations have learned to pray from this great prayer of the early Church, and this in the two directions proper to Christian prayer. For, as in the *Te Deum*, which has been called the twin of the Gloria, the first part of the hymn is directed to the Father, the second to Christ. The Gloria can also teach us something extremely important: the power that resides in self-forgetful praise of God the Father and of Christ. Nowhere else in our liturgy does this element of praise emerge so effectively as in the verse from the first part of the Gloria (the part addressed to the Father) that runs: "We worship you, we give you thanks, we praise you for your glory."

When the word "thank" is used, we would expect some

listing of God's blessings for which we are to thank him. But in this prayer we give thanks for something quite different: that God is so great and glorious. We forget not only what we want from God but even what we have received from him. Only one thing is important to us here; our thanksgiving is for one reason: that God exists and is so great and glorious.

If we understand the human heart even slightly, we know that this is how authentic love speaks: "I am so happy that you exist and are what you are." When this attitude does not reign between two lovers; when each is preoccupied only with what may be expected from the other; when weeks go by without a word of acknowledgment and appreciation, then love is dead. Lovers praise each other: that is the touchstone of all love.

Our prayer is liberating when, like this sentence in the Gloria, it constantly turns into self-forgetful, loving praise of God. It is as though we had sailed from the stifling air of the harbor into the refreshing breeze of the open sea; as though we climbed from the sultry valleys to the heights and the sharp, strong air that blows there. When the saints speak so ecstatically of the bliss of prayer that we "pedestrians" of the prayer life cannot follow them, they are thinking of the times when they have stood before God and, with or without words, have praised and thanked him for being so great and glorious.

*"We lift up
our heart to him
who is our head"*

14

WE HAVE OUR HEARTS WITH THE LORD

MANY people may have hoped that once the
faithful were permitted to sing and say their
parts of the Mass in the vernacular, various
key words and phrases in the celebration would impress
themselves unforgettably on their hearts. But the first
decade of a vernacular liturgy has already shown that this
will not happen unless the process is aided in some way.
The difficulty is that the key words and phrases in question
recur in the same form in every Mass; moreover, in keeping
with the general character of the Roman liturgy, they are
extremely reserved, so that tongue and heart may slip over
them unattentively.

One such key phrase that is repeated without change is the
response to the summons "Lift up your hearts" at the
beginning of the eucharistic prayer. It reads, in a literal
translation of the Latin: "We have them with the Lord."

Certain questions arise, however, when we reflect on this

venerable response of the congregation, a response which Christians in the Church of the martyrs uttered in the same form we use now.

Isn't it a bit late to be asking us at this point of the Mass to lift up our hearts? Shouldn't we be liberating our hearts from the thicket of daily cares at the very beginning of the Mass, in preparation for the penitential act, the readings and homily, and the intercessions? Shouldn't we be lifting up our hearts from the very beginning to him into whose presence we come when we enter the house of God?

By way of answer, I suggest that we must expand, in our minds, the summons to "lift up your hearts" that comes before the eucharistic prayer. The real sense of the summons is this: "If you have not done so already, it is high time that you lift up your hearts. For now we are entering together into the inner sanctuary of the celebration." This idea of a "last call" has not fully disappeared from our consciousness, as can be seen from the congregation's response: *"Habemus ad Dominum."* For the literal meaning of this short sentence is not: "We lift them up to the Lord," but, "We have them [i.e., already] with the Lord." The response that comes from the body of the Church is almost a mild reproach, as though the faithful were saying: "We've done long since what you are telling us to do now."

There is a second and more important question: Who is the Lord of whom we say that our hearts are with him? Is it the Father, to whom reference is made in the very next part of the dialogue as the addressee of our thanksgiving and to whom the entire eucharistic prayer is then directed? All indications suggest that this is not the correct answer. When interpreting the *Sursum corda* of the Mass, Augustine, who was the great champion of the idea that the eucharistic prayer has to be addressed to the Father, almost always understood Christ to be the "Lord" to whom we have lifted up our hearts: "We lift up our hearts to him who is our head." This is the basic idea that emerges from his paraphrases of the dialogue which introduces the eucharistic prayer.

An important aspect of eucharistic spirituality comes to the fore here. We must have our hearts with him who is being commemorated in the celebration; we must allow them to be drawn into the movement that is so wonderfully expressed at the other end of the eucharistic prayer, in the final doxology:

Through him, with him, in him . . .
all glory and honor is yours,
almighty Father,
for ever and ever.

How can we enter into this movement with Christ to the Father unless we have first accomplished ever anew the movement that lifts our hearts to Christ? One thing, however, is true of both movements: We cannot say "Abba, Father," or "Jesus is Lord," "except by the Holy Spirit" (1 Corinthians 12.3; cf. Romans 8.15).

"Those who, do not know the Gospel of Christ"

15

ALL WHO SEEK YOU WITH A SINCERE HEART

THESE words from the liturgy were the occasion of an unusual experience for me about a year and a half ago. During my vacation I celebrated evening Mass for a handful of visitors in the chapel of a charitable institution on a little island in the North Sea. In my introductory comments I said I would use the Fourth Eucharistic Prayer, and I asked the congregation to note how magnanimous the postconciliar Church has become in her prayer. In this eucharistic prayer she prays for all human beings who seek God with a sincere heart; concretely, this means that she prays even for Freemasons (it is hardly possible, is it, that there are none among them who seek God with a sincere heart?), as well as for Muslims and Buddhists, provided they are seeking God with a sincere heart.

39

Among those present at the Mass were a mother and her alert little seven-year-old daughter, Doris. A few days later the mother told me: "Can you imagine what Doris said to me the other evening after you had spoken of the Freemasons and the Buddhists? 'Mother,' she said, 'I think the priest saying Mass here now isn't a real priest. Otherwise he wouldn't have said that about the Freemasons. Only nice people get to heaven!' "

Are not many grownups infected with the narrow preconciliar mentality to which this child was giving expression? Have all of us become really convinced of what the Second Vatican Council finally said with such liberating clarity: "Those who, through no fault of their own, do not know the Gospel of Christ or his Church, but who nevertheless seek God with a sincere heart, and, moved by grace, try in their actions to do his will as they know it through the dictates of their conscience—those too may achieve eternal salvation" (*Dogmatic Constitution on the Church*, no. 16). The postconciliar Church is thus teaching us to open our hearts even in prayer and to include in our prayers at Mass all who "seek God with a sincere heart."

Among Catholics who have adopted this attitude there is no room for the bitter joke I once brought home with me from an ecumenical meeting. A newcomer to heaven was being taken on a tour by St. Peter; as they went, the person asked who were to be found in the space behind the high walls over which the singing of the Alleluia could be heard. "That's where we put the Catholics," St. Peter said. "We have to let them go on thinking there's no one else in heaven."

This kind of "belief" was always based on a misunderstanding; since the Council it has become untenable. It is an error and one that in addition causes pain, for in an unloving spirit it condemns and even, in the truest sense of the word, "damns" other human beings. We certainly desire and pray that each of the God-seekers for whom we pray at Mass will reach the full light of faith in Christ and his Church. But even if in God's unsearchable plan this does not happen, our prayer for them should then be even more fervent, because, when all is said and done, those who throughout their entire lives must follow their consciences without any conscious contact with Christ and without the Church and the sacraments, have it far more difficult than we do.

It is good then that at the very heart of her supreme liturgical celebration the praying Church should henceforth say: "Lord . . . remember . . . all [without exception] who seek you with a sincere heart."

16

FOR ALL THE DEAD
WHOSE FAITH IS KNOWN TO YOU ALONE

I N THE same Fourth Eucharistic Prayer in which the
Church prays with such striking magnanimity for all
who seek God with a sincere heart, the usual intercession for the dead is accompanied by a clause that should
really make every member of the Church sit up and take
notice because it is so extraordinary and so new in the
history of the Catholic liturgy. The praying Church here
commends to the Redeemer and his sacrifice even those of
the dead in whom their fellows could discern no sign of
faith. The text of this notable new intercession for the dead
runs thus: "Remember . . . all the dead whose faith is
known to you alone."

Beyond a doubt, the Church is here thinking of those whom
their neighbors, even the closest of them, regarded to the
end as unbelievers. The Church is saying: In the depths of

their hearts there may have been a faith which was visible only to the eyes of the all-seeing God. The Church rejoices, of course, when some reflection of the peace of Christ is to be seen on the faces of her dying members; and this kind of death in the peace of Christ is certainly one of the most wonderful things to be found on this earth. But how many people die quite differently every day: far removed from the faith of their childhood, and without having given any sign of faith during their last illness (to say nothing of cases of sudden death)!

Nothing makes the departure of dear ones so painful as their dying like that. It must therefore be a consolation to the survivors to have the praying Church admit the possibility that some last spark of faith may have glowed in the humanly invisible depths of such individuals.

Someone may say: "Isn't there at least one situation in which there is no basis for such a hope? I mean, of course, when in a final and fearful, because irreversible, act a man does violence to himself and takes his own life?"

Such an act is certainly an objectively serious sin against the One who alone has authority to decide the beginning and end of our life. But who can pass judgment on subjective guilt? Physicians tell us that there is hardly a single case of suicide in which mental illness does not play a part. And who can claim to know what happens in the final terrible minutes in the depths of a person who leaves life in this manner?

The Curé of Ars told an unconsolable widow whose husband had thrown himself from a bridge into the river: "Be comforted: God's mercy reached him between railing and water."

Thus it is that in the celebration of the redemptive sacrifice of Christ the Church does not exclude even suicides from her prayers. No one knows whether at the last moment when there was no turning back there flamed up in the hearts of these human beings a spark of faith, a spark of repentance, of which no one knew but God alone.

*The voice
not heard
in the streets*

17

TO YOU, MY GOD, I LIFT MY SOUL

A GOOD deal of thought certainly went into the choice of the words with which the Church begins the first Mass of her year: the Mass for the first Sunday of Advent. In some of our Sunday liturgies we do not hear the opening words of the Mass because we take advantage, on Sundays in particular, of our freedom to replace the entrance song of the Missal—the entrance antiphon—with vernacular hymns.

There are communities—and I can readily understand this—that would feel disoriented if this first Mass of Advent did not begin with an old familiar hymn like: "Drop down dew, ye heavens, from above." Anyone who hears the songs of this first Mass of the liturgical year as they are to be found in the Latin (and English) Missal cannot fail to be struck by the first two words of the entrance antiphon. In Latin each of these words contains only two letters, but at this point the short words are especially weighty. The words are *Ad te*: "To you, my God, I lift my soul." In the context there can be no doubt who is being addressed in these words from Psalm 25: the addressee is Christ.

To celebrate Advent means that in the dark depths of the year we open our hearts anew to him who is the true Sun of our life and whom we shall in a few weeks be celebrating as our Sun, when the time of the winter solstice comes around and with it the annual commemoration of the Redeemer's birth. We need a time of quiet in order to prepare for this feast, so that we may be able to hear the soft voice which so easily gets drowned out by the noise of the year, the voice of which the prophet had already said that it is not noisy and is not heard in the streets (Isaiah 42.2; Matthew 12.19).

Advent is a time for listening to this soft voice, a time in which we try to switch off to some extent the frightful noise that envelops us year in and year out. What Ambrose wrote in the fourth century is still true; in fact, it is truer than ever: "The devil wants noise, Christ wants stillness." When someone is trying to give us an important message on the telephone, we may find ourselves saying: "Excuse me a moment, I can't understand a word. Let me turn off the radio and close the door so that I won't hear the children shrieking. I'll be right back." In like manner we must "turn off" many sources of noise if we wish to hear the soft voice that has such important and consoling things to say to us. An Advent program of this kind is already set down for us in Psalm 85, which is an Advent psalm; it reads: "Let me hear what God the Lord will speak, for he will speak peace to his people, to his saints" (v. 8).

For evidence that we are on the right track when we thus interpret the two opening words of the entrance antiphon for the first Mass of Advent we may turn to an old choral office-book. In the expanded offertory song of this same Mass, the *Ad te* from Psalm 25 occurs again, and the one little word *te* has sixty-four notes! At work here is the holy irrationality of love that can never say "you" often enough. On the threshold of Advent, the Church, which is a bride, lifts up her hands and heart to the One, the bridegroom, who will come on his great Day to take her to his home.

Feastdays of our redemption

18

WITH THE INCARNATION OF YOUR SON OUR REDEMPTION HAS BEGUN

OUR first impression may be that Christmas and Easter do not have much to do with one another. Easter is marked by a certain austerity, whereas Christmas seems a "charming" time, and many people who no longer come to church even on Easter still come at Christmas. The happiness associated with the crèche and the Christmas carols touches their hearts. No one will scold them for this or accuse them of sentimentality, thus throwing cold water on the wick that still smolders there. Surely we do not want everything to turn to ice in their hearts!

But, whatever our impressions, the liturgy has always seen these two great feasts as forming a unity. Easter came first and for three hundred years was the only feast of Christ in the course of the year, each Sunday being a "little Easter" and reflecting the radiance of the annual feast. It was the feast in which the work of redemption was gratefully celebrated each year; it was the feast of our redemption through the death and resurrection of Christ.

In the fourth century the need was felt of an additional feast that would focus more directly on the person of the Redeemer. Arianism, the first heresy that threatened the entire world, had sought precisely to downgrade the divine dignity of the Redeemer. As a result, the feast which began to be celebrated on December 25 as the birthday of Christ, in place of a pagan feast of the sun's rebirth at the darkest time of year, remained closely associated with Easter. Christmas was thought of as the birthday not of the founder of a religion but of the Redeemer. This idea finds concise and striking expression in the prayer over the gifts at Midnight Mass: With the incarnation of your Son our redemption has begun. Jubilant though we are that he came, we cannot forget why he came: to rescue us by his death and resurrection.

The Christmas liturgy has retained something of the austere Easter tone, in order that we may remain aware that all feastdays of the Church are, in the final analysis, feastdays of our redemption. In fact, the liturgy does not hesitate to name and sing of the Redeemer's blood in the opening hymn (*Christus, Redemptor omnium*: Christ, Redeemer of all) of First Vespers on Christmas eve: "We too, redeemed by your holy blood, sing a new hymn for the day of your birth."

In the same spirit, even on Christmas all aspects of the feast converge in the sacrifice that calls our attention from Bethlehem to Jerusalem and the Supper Room and to the foot of the cross and the garden of the resurrection.

It is perfectly understandable, of course, that at Christmas the devotion of the people and especially of children should focus more sharply on the marvelous circumstances of this birth: stable and crib and shepherds and especially the mother of the divine child. No one would want to miss the precious Christmas carols and hymns at the crèche. It is good, nonetheless, that there be a heathy balance in the liturgy. It enables us to learn over and over again the ultimate all-embracing vision, so important in a world that is daily becoming more pagan, the comprehensive vision that can be summed up in a theological principle: All the feastdays of the Church (including Christmas and the feasts dedicated to individuals among the redeemed, especially Mary the first of the redeemed) are feastdays of our redemption.

Take
a pruning hook
to the tree

19

BY OUR BODILY FASTING
YOU GRANT US VIRTUE

"FASTING too has been dropped; we don't even dare call the Lenten season a 'season of fasting' any more." This is a complaint not infrequently heard in these years after the Council.

It is helpful to learn that this is one of the many misunderstandings people have of the real reform. It is not fasting that has been abrogated but (except for Good Friday and Ash Wednesday) only the strict law of fasting according to which any Catholic between twenty-one and sixty-five years of age may eat only one full meal a day on the weekdays of Lent. It was impossible to maintain that law any longer, if for no other reason than that the countless dispensations on account of health or work had created more and more exceptions to the rule. But the Church's urgent recommendation that we practice fasting, especially during the forty days before Easter, is still in effect.

This can be seen from the fact that the old Lenten Preface

49

with its praise of bodily fasting has been retained in the new Missal (as Preface IV of Lent). So, even after the Council, we hear in our churches: "By our bodily fasting you curb our vices, raise our minds, and grant us virtue and its rewards through Jesus Christ our Lord" (translation of the Latin text).

The Church remains convinced that the practice of fasting not only is good for the body (as physicians are discovering once again) but also opens the inner eye to the world above and to our neighbor and gives an unexpected measure of strength for loving God and neighbor, for praying, and for helping others.

The people of India tell us that by fasting we learn compassion. Lanza del Vasto, Gandhi's favorite European disciple, writes: "Those who are unwilling to let love of neighbor consume them are destined to stuff themselves with fine foods."

The Church reminds those who take advantage of the relaxed rules of fasting that Lent is to be a time of penance for them no less than for others. Besides, we all know full well that the forty days before Easter constitute not just any penitential season but one geared specifically to Easter.

At bottom, Christian fasting represents a serious effort to enter into the suffering death of Christ so as to share more fully in his Easter life. The Church does not preach abnegation for the sake of abnegation. In the spring of the year she bids us take a beneficial pruning hook to the tree, not because she wants the sharp cuts to bring pain to the tree, but because this painful action helps the tree blossom and bear fruit.

In any event, there is one point we must grasp clearly: All this activity does not mean that we can by our own powers bring about this interior conversion, this inner dying in order to live. The interior change is effected only by him of whom the preface in praise of fasting says: "You grant us virtue and its reward through Jesus Christ our Lord."

*Praise the Lord,
for great
is his mercy*

20

ALLELUIA

EACH year, when we reach the summit of the mountain that is Easter, the Easter Vigil echoes with a word that has not been spoken since Ash Wednesday but will accompany us through the liturgical year from now on. It is an unusual word that is not native to the English or even the Latin liturgical vocabulary: the word "Alleluia." As a matter of fact, it sounds less like a meaningful word than the babbling of a child, and when it is sung with many notes for the final vowel, this impression becomes even stronger.

"Alleluia" does, of course, have a meaning. It is a Hebrew word, and down the centuries the Church has brought it with her, untranslated (like "Amen"), as a product of the Jewish soil from which she herself sprang and as a reminder of her earliest days. The word is a cry of jubilation meaning "Praise the Lord," and occurs frequently in the psalms.

But the translation does not explain why the Church chose and retained this word from the Hebrew language of prayer in order to express her Easter jubilation, even though in later centuries her own children did not understand the meaning. I think the Church meant to say: "In the presence of the mystery that we celebrate on Easter, the mystery of our redemption, our usual intelligible vocabulary is inadequate; when faced with the superabundant mercy of God we can only stammer in amazement like children."

Our Alleluia, especially in developed musical form, is like the yodeling of an Alpine shepherd, who at daybreak sees the morning sun touch the snowy peak with the first delicate tint of rose. The feelings in the shepherd's heart at this moment cannot be expressed in well-chosen words he may have learned in school; he must yodel his feelings.

That is how it is with us Christians: As we gaze at the Sun that has risen high over the darkness and cold of our Good Friday, all well-chosen words are useless. We can only stammer out our Alleluia of wonder and jubilation. Christ, our true morning Sun, has risen from the darkness of the tomb; the hour is at hand when brightness and warmth fill even the valleys where it is still Good Friday.

It is wonderful to think that this Easter cry of jubilation has accompanied the Church since the days of her childhood; that amid all the ups and downs of almost two thousand years it has been sung over and over again on this night of nights, in the cathedrals and village churches of the entire world, in the certainty that he whom we praise will be with the Church until he comes again on the clouds of heaven.

True enough, in the world in which we live there seems reason for everything but the singing of Alleluia. And yet this is the basic hope to which our faith gives us access: that for us as for Christ Good Friday is not a goal but a way station. You may remember that "Pasch," the old name for Easter, has its exact English translation in the name for the Jewish Easter: "Passover." Because we know that our entire life is but a "passing over" to the city of God in which "all her lanes will cry 'Hallelujah' " (Tobit 13.18), therefore, even now amid the darkness of our Good Friday, we can sing "Alleluia—Praise the Lord, for great is his mercy." He intends to lead us, his members, along the victorious way that he himself has traveled through death to life.

signs
gestures and
words

interpreted for children

A sign of our baptism

1

WHY DO WE TAKE HOLY WATER AS WE ENTER A CHURCH?

DEAR CHILDREN! The first time your mother came to church with you, she showed you what you should do as you entered the house of God. You dipped your fingers into the holy water font (or, if it was too high for you, she reached into it for you and passed the holy water to you on her fingertips), and then slowly made the sign of the cross on yourself from forehead to breast and from left shoulder to right; you then genuflected toward the Blessed Sacrament and entered the pew. That's rather complicated, I admit; when you enter a movie house, you make your way to your seat much more quickly!

But then, dear children, a church is not a movie house. It is a dwelling unlike any other. We call it the Lord's house, because it is consecrated to the one Lord to whom everything belongs. The holy Body of the Lord is reverently kept in it, if for no other reason than that it might be there and be able to be brought quickly if a dying person suddenly needs Viaticum. You all know how to tell whether and where the Body of the Lord is kept in a church: a little red light burns, as a sign of the Lord's presence, in front of the tabernacle in which the Blessed Sacrament is kept. Because this lamp burns day and night, it is sometimes called the "perpetual light."

I do not want to talk to you today about all the things we do as we enter a church, but only about one: the taking of holy water. Why do we use water as we enter the church? The reason for it is not very obvious, is it?

It is true that water is "not necessary" at the entrance of a church. The water is rather a sign. It is intended to remind us of that other water without which no one enters the great Church that is built not of stones but of living human beings. You have belonged to this Catholic Church since your earliest days, and you did not become a member of it without water, the water of baptism.

Every time, then, that we enter a house of God, we should gratefully remind ourselves: "I am baptized, and therefore this house is my house. The Body that is kept up there where the tabernacle lamp is burning has been my food since the day of my first communion. I must behave with reverence in this house of God (no basketball playing here, no roller skating), because it is the Lord's house. Just the same, I am not a stranger in this house; it is the house of *my* Lord, because I am baptized."

Perhaps you've been present when the priest blesses the holy water before Mass on Sunday (the water is then put in the holy water basins at the doors of the church). And if the blessing took place in the Easter season, you heard the priest say just what we've been talking about here today. As he made the sign of the cross over the water he said: "Lord, bless this water so that it will be for us a sign of the baptism we have received." Amen.

When you wish to pray, shut the door

2

WHY DOES THE PRIEST PAUSE AFTER THE WORDS "LET US PRAY"?

DEAR CHILDREN! Recently little Ruth returned home from the children's Mass and said: "Momma, something's wrong with our priest. Every time he says 'Let us pray' at Mass, he suddenly stops and says nothing for a while. What's the matter with him?"

Her mother said: "Well, just think for a moment. We do almost the same thing here at home when we say grace at table. When you children want to rush into the prayer, I always tell you: Put your dolls aside for a while; turn off the trains; no more noise or giggling. Let's be still for a moment. We're going to do something very different, something much more important than playing. We're going to pray."

That's what your priest is saying to you. Of course, you don't have your trains or dolls in church with you, but maybe your thoughts are still at home with your toys or your chores or a thousand other things. If they are, you can't just start praying. If you did, you would take with you all the distractions that are useless when you pray. The priest is saying to the people: "Let us pull ourselves together." He doesn't mean that in these few moments of silence the people should already be really praying. They should be thinking: "Now we must put everything else aside. Only one thing is important now—the great living God with whom we are to speak."

I think that Ruth's mother gave the right explanation and that from then on Ruth understood better the "funny pauses" of the priest. I have another example that can help show what is going on. I was recently in a great cathedral in France. To enter it, I first had to climb a long majestic set of stairs, but even then I was not in the cathedral. I still had to pass through a wide, deep doorway with old statues of saints on its wall; I had to pull open a heavy oak door. Only then was I inside and could hear the people singing Morning Prayer very beautifully, in French, before Mass.

Now, why did the old architects make things so complicated with stairs and doorways? They could have made the entrance much simpler. They could have just put a big opening in the wall up toward the front; then people could come directly from the marketplace into the interior of the church. But the builders knew that this would not be good for people, because they would have brought all the commotion of the marketplace into church with them. The long journey up the stairs and through the doorway would give them the time to gather their thoughts. They could say to themselves: "It is time now to forget everything outside and all the things we still have to do out there. Only one thing is important now: we must pray."

Dear children! Jesus once said: "When you wish to pray, go to your room and shut the door." That is what the priest is saying to the people when, after urging them "Let us pray," he stops for a moment. He is saying: "First, shut the door of your heart so that you won't hear all the noise outside. Things must become still, outside and inside you. Then together we can come before the living God; then we can begin to pray to him." Amen.

Speak, Lord,
I am listening

3

WHY DO WE STAND FOR THE GOSPEL AND MAKE THE SIGN OF THE CROSS?

DEAR children! Have you ever attended a solemn Mass celebrated by a bishop? If you have, you must have been struck by all the ceremony that accompanied the reading of the gospel. The deacon went to the altar, took the book of gospels from it, and went to the bishop for a blessing. Then in solemn procession with an incense-bearer and two candle-bearers he carried the book of gospels to the lectern. When he reached it, all the people in the church stood up. Then while singing the words of the introduction he made a sign of the cross on the gospel book and then on his forehead, his lips, and his breast, and the congregation did the same. Next, he incensed the book of gospels, and only then did he begin to read it. At the end, too, he did something special: before all the people he kissed the book from which he had just been reading.

Now that is really a lot of ceremonial, especially when you recall that the previous passages of scripture had simply been read aloud! We must therefore reflect and ask why the gospel reading is so special. Some points of the answer are important for you yourselves, as you will see in a moment.

At your usual Sunday Masses there is not so much ceremony connected with the gospel. But there are two things you have taken for granted ever since you first attended Sunday Mass with your parents: you stand for this part of the Mass, and at the beginning of the gospel you make a sign of the cross with your thumb on your forehead, lips, and breast. We must ask: What is the reason for these actions?

The gospel is the only one of the readings in which Jesus himself speaks. Over and over we hear: "But Jesus said." Then his own words ring through the church and reach the ears of modern listeners. All the ceremonial that I spoke of springs from reverence for the one who speaks here. If the bishop were to appear in your religion class, you would all leap to your feet without being told. How much more, then, should we stand when the one whom the bishop only represents himself enters the assembly! The sign of the cross on forehead, lips, and heart also has to do with this Lord who is entering the assembly and will now speak. Everyone present is saying as it were: "Now I must pay attention. It is my Lord who speaks. Since my baptism I have belonged to him body and soul, in my thoughts, words, and feelings."

Recently a young Protestant boy was a visitor at a Catholic children's liturgy. Afterwards, he asked his Catholic classmates: "At one point all of you suddenly moved your hand over your face. What was that about?" The question showed that the Catholic children must have been making this sign of the cross too rapidly and negligently. Perhaps they did not realize all that we have been thinking about here today. Anyone who does realize it can only make the three signs of the cross very slowly and reverently, and think meanwhile: "Jesus, I belong to you. Speak, Lord, I am listening." Amen.

The letter
from heaven

WHY DOES THE PRIEST
KISS THE GOSPEL BOOK?

DEAR children! Certainly at one time or another you have heard your grandfather or grandmother say, "The children will drive me crazy with their constant question: Why? They wish to know everything, even things they cannot understand at all as yet." However, you really have a right to ask. Grown-ups are there to explain to you many puzzling things, found on this earth, if these things can be explained at all.

It is no different in the Church. There one sees many things that seem strange and one would like to ask: Why? For example, just now before I laid down the gospel book I kissed it. You see that done each time a priest or a deacon reads the gospel. And you would like to ask: Why is the book kissed?

I want to explain this to you, dear children. Kissing has

something to do with loving. Your mother kisses your little sister or brother and sometimes she kisses you, too, because she loves you. The groom kisses his bride as a sign of his love for her. Thus kissing the gospel book must have something to do with love and I believe here we are on the right track. We need only think a little more about what kind of a book it is the priest kisses. The great and holy Church Father Augustine once said that the Bible is a letter, which God himself has written us to comfort us on our earthly pilgrimage.

Even a letter from a human being can be a real comfort to us. During the last war I knew a young girl who was engaged. Her fiancé had to go to Russia. At first a letter came from him every few days. Then nothing came for a week, even for two weeks. All at once, after a whole month, the mailman came waving a letter at a distance. Her fiancé had really written; she knew he was alive! Can you understand that the girl kissed the letter for joy before she opened it? The kiss was not intended for the envelope or the postage stamps but for him who had written the letter and for whatever he wrote after such a long silence.

I once attended a Mass for Christians who were exiled from Russia. There the priest, after kissing the gospel book himself, passed it around to the people to kiss. I recall very well how he lifted the book up high, so that a very little boy, carried on his father's arms, could kiss it. You see, not only the priest is happy with this book, for the letter from heaven is intended not only for him. It is intended for all of us. For that reason we read from it at each Mass.

Even though we cannot introduce the practice here of letting everyone kiss the gospel book, all of us should think what the priest thinks when he kisses the book: Thank God that among millions of books we have this one book in which God himself speaks to us again and again. It is the letter of our heavenly Father to his children who are still traveling toward heaven.

In your Son
we offer you
a pleasing sacrifice

5

WHY DOES THE PRIEST RAISE HOST AND CHALICE BEFORE THE OUR FATHER, AND WE ALL ANSWER "AMEN"?

DEAR children! If you pay close attention at Mass, you have surely been struck by the moment when the priest takes the chalice in his right hand and the plate with the hosts on it in his left, raises both aloft, and sings aloud: "Through him [he means: Through Christ] and with him and in him . . . all glory and honor is yours, almighty Father, for ever and ever." Then you all join in answering the priest with "Amen." Where does this moment come in the Mass? Not before the consecration, for at that time it is still only bread that lies on the altar, and still only wine that fills the chalice. What the priest raises aloft is the transformed bread and the transformed wine, that is, the body and blood of Christ, and he does it at the end of the great eucharistic prayer that began with "The Lord be with you. . . . Lift up your hearts." Immediately after the raising of the hosts and the chalice comes the Our Father in which we prepare ourselves for communion.

What is the priest saying in this final prayer and the elevation of the gifts? We might express it this way: "What I hold in my hands and raise aloft is the precious gifts which we are allowed to offer the heavenly Father in the Mass. Of ourselves we have nothing, but in our empty hands he has put the body and blood of his Son who surrendered himself to death for our sakes."

All of you sing "Amen" in response to the priest. What do you mean by this word? "Amen" is a Hebrew word, and the Church has brought it with her from her first home, from the land and language of the Jews. It has the same meaning here as our little English word "Yes." For it is not only the priest but all of us with the priest and with one another who bring this marvelous gift into God's presence in order to praise and glorify him: "All honor and glory is yours, almighty Father."

Dear children! You understand better now how important the little word "Amen" is at this point in the Mass. St. Jerome tells us that in his day the faithful of Rome sang it so loudly and fervently that it echoed like thunder from the walls of the old churches. I was recently present in a cathedral for a solemn episcopal Mass at which some new priests were ordained. Here the Amen was sung no less than seven times: once by the congregation, then three times by a cantor, and finally three times by the congregation again. On that occasion, too, the Amen echoed like heavenly thunder from the walls of the old cathedral. You could sense what the people meant to say: "Yes! This is the sacrifice of us all that rises before the face of God; it is the praise and thanksgiving and petitions of us all."

In our children's Masses when you sing the Amen, someone entering the church at this moment must surely realize what you are expressing: "Yes, these sacrificial gifts which the priest up there holds in his hands and raises aloft are our gifts too. Receive them, Lord!" Amen.

67

OUR FATHER...

6

WHY IS THE OUR FATHER
OFTEN SUNG AT MASS?

DEAR children! All of you know what a great prayer the Our Father is, because Jesus himself gave it to the human race. To his disciples and to all of us he says: "This is how you are to pray."

We might think that so important a prayer, in which all our requests of God are summed up, should always be spoken by the people: spoken slowly and solemnly, yes, but not sung! If someone were to be received by the president of our country and allowed to present requests, he would speak what he had to say, slowly and calmly; it would be quite strange if he were to sing his requests to the president. Yet that is just what we do, not always but often, at the Our Father of the Mass. What about this? Isn't it really rather comical?

I want to tell you of a little experience that may perhaps help us here. I once saw a small group of children burst with joyous shouts from a schoolhouse. (You know the kind of thing I mean: there's a sigh of relief if the children do not fall over one another, since they can't get down the steps fast enough.) A teacher had fallen ill, and the summer vacation was beginning two days early for this class. As the children ran down the street, they tossed their schoolbags in the air and sang over and over: "We're on vacation! We're on vacation!"

Now they could just as well have spoken or shouted (or even shrieked) these few words. Why, then, did these children want to sing them? You've guessed the answer: Because they were so happy! For pure joy they could not help singing. They had to sing out their joy. That's how it is with us when we approach God as our Father. We suddenly feel joy; we realize how marvelous it is to have a real Father in heaven who is as kind and strong and affectionate as our father at home, and even much, much more so: a Father to whom we can confidently tell what is on our mind. We are not crying out into an emptiness; we know that in heaven there is indeed a loving Father who hears and answers us and who is ready to give us our true daily bread and forgive our sins and rescue us from evil.

I wonder whether you have ever thought about why the Our Father comes at this particular place in the celebration and not, for example, at the beginning or the end of Mass. You might think it would fit in very well at these points. But instead we speak or sing it every time we prepare for communion. I want to tell you why this has been the practice at Mass for over a thousand years. Right after the Lord's Prayer we personally experience the fact that God is a loving Father who answers our prayers. No sooner have we prayed to him: "Give us our daily bread," than he uses the priest's hand to place holy bread in our own hand (or on our tongue): not ordinary bread but bread that has been mysteriously changed into the body of his Son, the most precious of all the gifts we may receive from the hand of God.

It's understandable, isn't it, that for pure joy we should want to sing so great and rich a prayer as this, a prayer so quickly and marvelously answered? We sing for the same reason that the children on the street that day sang "We're on vacation! We're on vacation!": we sing for pure joy. Amen.

At this table
we are all
brothers and sisters

7

WHY DO WE OFFER A SIGN OF PEACE TO ONE ANOTHER BEFORE COMMUNION?

DEAR children! You now take it for granted that at every school Mass there comes a moment, shortly before communion, when the priest invites you to give a sign of peace to your neighbor to right and left, and you usually shake hands. I notice that on each occasion this greeting of peace makes you very happy.

How would we explain this gesture to other children who have so far not practiced it? I think we could explain it this way. You would say to them: "You've attended a big family dinner, haven't you? You've seen how guests who didn't even know each other or hadn't seen each other for a long time shook hands before taking their place at the table. No one thinks of staring at his plate and looking neither right nor left, but just saying: 'What do I care about the other guests? When will I get a real dinner to eat?'"

Holy communion is like a big family dinner; in fact, it is the most wonderful feast in the world. You often hear the priest saying, just before communion, as he holds the host in his hand: "This is the Lamb of God who takes away the sins of the world. Happy are those who are called to his supper." It cannot be a matter of indifference to us who else is invited to this wedding feast. Here you must greet your neighbor and say to him, as it were: "How wonderful that you too have been invited to his holy table and that we may eat this holy food together!"

At big outdoor Masses there are often thousands of people present. There are loudspeakers all around the place, so that everyone can hear what is going on at the altar; they can think and pray and sing in unison. I read an account written by a woman who had been present at one of these Masses. She wrote: "I had an experience at this Mass that I will never forget, even if I live to be a hundred. In the milling crowd I did not notice who was standing next to me. When the call came over the loudspeakers before communion: 'Now let us shake hands with our neighbor as a sign of peace,' I suddenly saw a black hand clasping my white hand. An African woman had been standing near me unnoticed. Then it struck me how right this handshake before communion is. At this table we are all brothers and sisters, and become more so each time."

Dear children! You can now understand why on many occasions, you can pray a little prayer that runs something like this: "Jesus Christ, Savior and Redeemer, once again you have invited all of us together at your table. Help us to be kind to one another as if we were all brothers and sisters. For you really made us your brothers and sisters when you gave your body to death for our sakes." Amen.

You call me by name

8

DEAR children! Couldn't priests and other eucharistic ministers make it a lot simpler when they have to distribute communion to a great many people? Before beginning the distribution they could elevate a host at the altar and say aloud, just once: "The body of Christ," and all in the church could answer: "Amen." Then the sacrament could be silently placed in the hand or on the tongue of each individual. Instead of this simple procedure, the minister must repeatedly say (often a hundred times over), to each successive communicant: "The body of Christ," and each communicant personally gives the same answer: "Amen." There must be a reason for making things so complicated.

The answer to this question is simple but important. The purpose of conducting this little dialogue with each communicant is to make us understand that in the sacrament Jesus comes to each individual and considers each individual to be as important as if he or she were the only person in the world. It is right, therefore, that the individual should profess faith in this mystery. What the priest is saying is: "What I am giving you here is the body of Christ," and the individual answers: "Amen," which amounts to saying: "Yes, I believe that."

In Russia, when Christians come to communion, each person, adult or child, whispers his or her first name to the priest, who then says: "Andrew, servant of God, receives the body of the Lord," or "Elizabeth, handmaid of God, receives the body of the Lord."

It is as though Jesus were calling by name those who come to him, just as he called a tearful Mary Magdalene by name in the garden on Easter morning. You know the story: how she first thought the stranger was the gardener, until he spoke her name: "Mary!"; then she knew that it was Jesus and cried: "Teacher!", threw herself at his feet, and tried to cling to him for sheer joy.

Jesus lovingly calls by name each person to whom he bends down in the mystery of holy communion. He knows each of us better than we know ourselves.

When I recently spoke this last sentence to some children, I thought to myself, "Perhaps that's a bit difficult for them to grasp," and so I added: "When you grow up you'll understand this short sentence fully." But a little girl raised her hand and said: "I already understand it. He made us, and so he must know what's in us."

Yes, dear children, the Bible says almost word for word what the little girl said: "Jesus knew what was in man" (John 2.25). He knows our heart, and every time he comes to us, he says to each of us what the prophet Isaiah wrote: "Fear not . . . I have called you by name, you are mine." Amen.

Look!
your king is
coming to you!

9

WHY DO WE LAY OUR LEFT HAND
ON OUR RIGHT WHEN WE RECEIVE
THE BODY OF CHRIST?

DEAR children! If you wish to receive holy communion in the hand, this is how you do it. Slowly and with joined hands you come forward to the place where it is being distributed. When your turn comes, the minister shows you the host and says: "The body of Christ." You answer aloud and in a clear voice: "Amen." Then you place your left hand, palm up, on the right, and the host is placed on it. You take a short step to the side, stop for a moment, and with your right hand reverently take host from your left hand and place it in your mouth. Then, with hands joined, you return quietly to your place.

I don't know whether you remember what the unusual placing of one hand on the other is intended to mean. This manner of receiving the Lord's body is extremely ancient; even sixteen hundred years ago the people were instructed to receive in this way, and they were told the reason for it. They were to form a kind of throne with their hands and to receive the heavenly king on it: the right hand is the base of the throne, and the left forms the seat. They were not to be afraid that one of these two "sisters"—the right and left hands—might be jealous of the other, for, after all, the right hand too helps support the body of the king.

This, then, is the point of thus laying one hand on top of the other. It is as though the eucharistic minister had told you: "Look! your king is coming to you!" and you answered: "Yes, and I build a throne for him with my hands, a little altar of my own." You will recall that the altar has always been described as the throne of Christ; that is why we honor it and decorate it.

You can also understand now, dear children, why it is not proper to reach for the host with thumb and forefinger; the image of a throne is lost, and the degree of reverence is not the same. I recently heard of a boy who told someone: "I couldn't go to communion yesterday. As I was coming up I suddenly saw that my hands were very dirty; we had been playing football before Mass." The boy was right in feeling that one should not offer a dirty hand as a throne for the king of heaven and earth. But he didn't stop to think that he can always receive communion in the old way, on the tongue; his tongue was surely not dirty from playing football!

Dear children! Cooperate in seeing to it that the communion procession takes place very peacefully. Haste is always out of place (you know that from watching traffic), but here it is doubly out of place. Anyone who reflects even briefly on who it is that he receives in his hand and into his heart, will grow silent and peaceful from sheer reverence and joy. "Look! your king is coming to you!" Amen.

We turn
our souls
to the sun

10

WHY IS THE FIRST DAY OF THE WEEK CALLED "SUNDAY"?

DEAR children! You surely learned in school that Sunday takes its name from the sun. Our ancestors gave it this name long before they became Christians. The name was current when the first Christian missionaries told the people: "The day of the week that you call 'Sunday' is one that you must keep holy more than any other day; each Sunday you must gather to celebrate the memory of the Redeemer, for on this day he rose gloriously from the dead."

Now you may be surprised that the missionaries did not go a step further and say: "For this reason we would like this day to have another name from now on; for example, we might call it 'Christ-day.' " Let me explain to you why the missionaries did not do this. They thought to themselves: It is better to let the people go on using the old name, but to give it a new meaning. That was very easy to do with this particular name, because Christ himself had said: "I am the light of the world," which amounted to saying: "I am the sun of the world." Therefore the missionaries told the people: "Continue to use your old name for this day. But when you use it, think of another sun: the Sun that rose from the tomb in Jerusalem on Easter morning, and since that day has been shining on all who believe in him. Let Sun-day mean Christ-day to you."

As a matter of fact, when thus understood, "Sunday" is really the most beautiful name we can think of for the first day of the week. It is the day on which Christ, our true Sun, rose from the tomb. That is why it is so obvious and necessary that we gather around the altar where Christ is our sacrificial lamb and Easter lamb and where he invites us to his sacrificial meal, his Easter banquet.

A missionary once asked a young African convert who used to spend long hours kneeling before the tabernacle without a book in his hands (in fact, the boy could not even read): "What do you do for such long periods?" He received a marvelous answer: "I turn my soul to the sun." That is what we do each Sunday when we come to Mass and communion: we turn our souls to the sun. Then they are enlightened and warmed by the light of Christ.

Dear children, do you know one of the reasons why so many people today are usually morose and out of sorts and depressed and dissatisfied? They do not observe Sunday any more. They have—or say they have—no time to attend church on Sunday. They no longer know what it means and how beneficial it is to turn one's soul to the sun. Where there is no sun, there is no joy.

There are people who live in deep Alpine valleys into which the sun does not penetrate at all for a few days or even a few weeks of the year. Just ask such people what really depressing days are! An old pastor in the Tyrol told me he'd been a curate in such a valley. One morning, when the sun shone into the school window for the first time after nine sunless days, the good Tyrolean children suddenly climbed on to their seats and shouted for sheer joy. Our joy on Sundays doesn't express itself so loudly, but we can nevertheless compare it with the joy that burst forth that morning in the Tyrolean schoolroom. The true Sun of our life rises over us on the day we call "Sun-day," and we are able to turn our souls to this Sun. How can we fail to rejoice in it? Amen.